Who Was
Harriet Beecher Stowe?

Who Was
Harriet Beecher Stowe?

By Dana Meachen Rau

Illustrated by Gregory Copeland

Grosset & Dunlap
An Imprint of Penguin Group (USA) LLC

For my Tuesday Morning Writers
and their powerful words—DMR

To my mother, Carole—GC

GROSSET & DUNLAP
Published by the Penguin Group
Penguin Group (USA) LLC, 375 Hudson Street, New York, New York 10014, USA

USA | Canada | UK | Ireland | Australia | New Zealand | India | South Africa | China

penguin.com
A Penguin Random House Company

Text copyright © 2015 by Dana Meachen Rau. Illustrations copyright © 2015 by Penguin Group (USA) LLC. All rights reserved. Published by Grosset & Dunlap, a division of Penguin Young Readers Group, 345 Hudson Street, New York, New York 10014. GROSSET & DUNLAP is a trademark of Penguin Group (USA) LLC. Printed in the USA.

Library of Congress Cataloging-in-Publication Data is available.

ISBN 978-0-448-48301-6   10 9 8 7 6 5 4 3 2 1

Contents

Who Was
Harriet Beecher Stowe?

During the 1800s, the economy of the southern United States boomed with the production of cotton. Many white plantation owners became rich growing it. They relied on black slaves to work their fields and harvest the cotton. These slaves were not treated as people. They were property to buy and sell, just like livestock or farm equipment.

In 1850, the US Congress passed the Fugitive Slave Act. It stated that anyone caught giving food, shelter, or help of any kind to an escaped slave would have to pay a $1,000 fine and spend six months in jail. The people of the United States had long been divided over the issue of slavery. This new law meant that even those who were against slavery could offer no help. If they assisted runaway slaves in any way, they would be breaking the law. Slaves who managed to escape to the North could not be protected.

When this law passed, Harriet Beecher Stowe was a writer and mother, living in Brunswick, Maine. She and her family had long been against slavery. But she was especially horrified by stories she heard of slave owners forcibly taking back slaves who had escaped to freedom. No black man, woman, or child was safe.

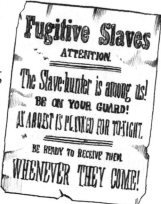

Harriet's sister-in-law wrote to her saying, "Hattie, if I could use a pen as you can, I would write something to make this whole nation feel what an accursed thing slavery is!" After reading the letter, Harriet got up from her chair, crushed the paper in her hands, and declared, "I will write something. I will if I live."

Harriet Beecher Stowe went on to write one of the most famous books in US history, *Uncle Tom's Cabin*. She worried that no one would listen to what she had to say.

But they did.

Uncle Tom's Cabin was not only an instant success. It changed the course of history. Harriet's book revealed the horrors of slavery. It fueled the tensions that led to the Civil War.

Her words helped inspire people to change. Her story helped bring an end to slavery in the United States.

Chapter 1
A Busy Household

Harriet Beecher was born on June 14, 1811, in the small New England town of Litchfield, Connecticut. Her father, Reverend Lyman Beecher, had hoped for a boy whom he wanted to name Henry. But his wife, Roxana, gave birth to a girl instead. They chose to name her Harriet, and called her Hattie for short.

The house was already quite full of children when Hattie became the sixth child in the Beecher household. After Hattie, Roxana had two more boys. Hattie was always surrounded by family. Her grandmother and aunt lived right down a garden path from her own house. Because Hattie's father was a Congregational minister in town, the Beecher house on the upper end of North Street was often filled with visitors.

The family suffered a great loss when Hattie was only five. Her mother died of tuberculosis in September 1816. Later in life, Harriet wrote: "I remember the mourning dresses, the tears of the older children, the walking to the burial ground, and somebody's speaking at the grave . . . we little ones, to whom it was so confused, asked the question where she was gone and would she ever come back?"

Lyman thought it might be good for Hattie to escape the sadness of the household. Hattie went to live with her other grandmother, aunt, and uncle in Nut Plains, Connecticut. The night Hattie arrived, the outside of their home struck her as a "lonely little white farmhouse." But her worries calmed when she entered the parlor, where a cozy fire crackled in welcome.

Here, Aunt Harriet turned all of her attention onto little Hattie. She taught Hattie how to knit and sew. She taught her manners and prayers.

Hattie spent her time memorizing hymns, poems, and quotes from the Bible. She was intrigued by the treasures around the house brought back by her uncle, Samuel Foote, a sea captain. The house was filled with exotic items, such as fabrics from India, bells from China, and incense from Spain. Hattie stayed in Nut Plains for almost a year before she returned to her family in Litchfield.

Back at home, the household didn't go without a mother for long. Lyman was preaching in Boston when he met another Harriet—Miss Harriet Porter. They married in the fall of 1817. Hattie remembered the night her new mother arrived in Litchfield. Hattie was sharing a bedroom with her younger brothers when she met her for the first time. She later wrote, "A beautiful lady, very fair, with bright blue eyes, and soft auburn hair . . . came into the room smiling, eager, and happy-looking . . . and told us that she loved little children, and that she would be our mother."

Lyman and Harriet Porter had two more children together while in Litchfield.

Hattie grew up in a very religious home. Her father was a powerful, energetic, and famous preacher. He believed that people were born sinful and needed to pray to God to save them so they could enter heaven when they died. Lyman was determined to save souls—both in his congregation and elsewhere.

Throughout New England, he was called to help lead revival events. He was strict with his children and required them to obey him. He did not believe in the rituals of other branches of Christianity, such as celebrating Easter and Christmas.

Even though Lyman was busy as a spiritual leader in their community, he still made time to play with his children. The Beecher family was happy and supportive of one another.

Hattie later wrote that she was raised in "a great household inspired by a spirit of cheerfulness and hilarity." The family chopped wood together and shook chestnuts from trees. They gathered in the kitchen to peel apples for apple butter in the fall.

While they worked, their father asked questions and led debates. He entertained them with pranks and by playing the fiddle. At a time when girls were not given as many opportunities as boys, the Beecher family, full of both boys and girls, treated one another equally.

When Hattie had a moment alone, she could be found with a book. Her father's study was one of her favorite rooms. "High above all the noise of the house," she wrote, "this room had to me the air of a refuge and a sanctuary.

Its walls were set round from floor to ceiling with the friendly, quiet faces of books." She would sit in the corner of this room reading while her father wrote at his desk. Searching for more to read one day, she riffled through a barrel where her father kept his sermons. Underneath the old papers, she found a copy of *Arabian Nights*, a collection of folktales from Asia and the Middle East. She treasured it and read it over and over again.

Lyman preferred that Hattie only read religious books. He called novels "trash" and considered them evil. But Uncle Samuel had traveled the world and seen many cultures. He liked reading stories himself and convinced Lyman to change his mind. Hattie's father finally gave in. Poetry and novels became a part of the Beecher household, and Hattie read whatever she could get her hands on.

THE FAMOUS BEECHER FAMILY

LYMAN BEECHER (1775-1863) HAD A LARGE FAMILY, AND HE EXPECTED ALL OF HIS CHILDREN TO BE ACTIVE MEMBERS OF SOCIETY. MANY OF HIS CHILDREN, INCLUDING HARRIET, CATHARINE, CHARLES, AND EDWARD, BECAME PUBLISHED AUTHORS. ALL SEVEN OF HIS SONS BECAME MINISTERS.

LYMAN BEECHER

CATHARINE BEECHER (1800-1878) WAS AN EDUCATOR AND ACTIVIST WHO CHAMPIONED EDUCATION FOR WOMEN AND THE IMPORTANCE OF KINDERGARTEN FOR CHILDREN.

CATHARINE BEECHER

HENRY WARD BEECHER (1813-1887) WAS A FAMOUS PREACHER AND SPEAKER KNOWN FOR SUPPORTING THE ABOLITION OF SLAVERY.

HENRY WARD
BEECHER

ISABELLA BEECHER HOOKER (1822-1907) WAS A VOICE FOR WOMEN'S RIGHTS AND SUFFRAGE (THE RIGHT TO VOTE) AND LOBBIED CONGRESS TO CHANGE UNFAIR LAWS.

ISABELLA BEECHER
HOOKER

Chapter 2
Student and Teacher

In the early 1800s, Litchfield, Connecticut, was a center of culture and learning. Many politicians, lawyers, and poets lived there. Litchfield also had two famous schools. One was Judge Tapping Reeve's Litchfield Law School for college-age men. The other was Miss Sarah Pierce's Litchfield Female Academy. Girls from age eight into their

LITCHFIELD FEMALE ACADEMY

early twenties attended Miss Pierce's—one of the first schools for girls in the country. The schools didn't have dormitories, so students rented rooms from people in town. The Beecher household took in students as boarders.

When Harriet turned eight, she started attending the famous Litchfield Female Academy. It was an easy walk from home. The same subjects were taught as at boys' schools, including Latin, geography, math, science, and grammar. One of its teachers, Mr. John Brace, made a big impact on Harriet.

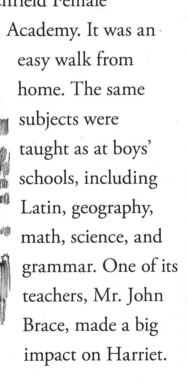

To Harriet, he was "one of the most stimulating and inspiring instructors I ever knew." She wrote many essays for him.

At the end of the school year in 1824, Mr. Brace selected her essay to be read aloud at the academy's annual exhibition. Harriet was only thirteen. Lyman Beecher was so impressed that afterward he asked Mr. Brace who had written it. He was delighted to learn it was his own daughter!

Harriet was equally glad. "It was the proudest moment of my life," she later wrote. "There was no mistaking father's face when he was pleased, and to have interested him was past all juvenile triumphs."

In the 1800s, women's roles were slowly
beginning to change. Rather than relying on
their husbands and the males in their households
to make decisions for them, women were looking
for ways to become more independent. Schools
called seminaries opened for women to prepare
them for professional lives as teachers or lives as
mothers. Women lobbied the government for
the right to own property. They rallied around
the issue of suffrage—women's right to vote.

Harriet grew up in a family that supported the education of women and sought their opinions on issues of the day.

Harriet's oldest sister, Catharine, had started her own school in Hartford, Connecticut. Catharine Beecher's Hartford Female Seminary opened in the spring of 1823 with only seven students. After the school's successful first year, Catharine wanted Harriet to study there, too.

Girls at seminaries usually started at age fifteen and attended classes for one to three years. But Harriet was only thirteen when she ventured thirty miles to Hartford by stagecoach. The school was housed in one room above the White Horse harness shop. Students boarded with nearby families.

The Bull family took in Harriet in exchange for their daughter staying with the Beechers in Litchfield to attend Miss Pierce's school. After growing up in such a busy household, Harriet was quite pleased that "a neat little hall chamber was allotted to me for my own."

THE CONGREGATIONAL CHURCH

THE BEGINNINGS OF CONGREGATIONALISM IN NEW ENGLAND STARTED WITH THE ARRIVAL OF COLONISTS FROM ENGLAND IN THE 1600S.

THESE NEW SETTLERS, CALLED PURITANS, WANTED TO BREAK AWAY FROM THE TRADITIONS OF THE CHURCH OF ENGLAND. THEY SETTLED IN PRESENT-DAY MASSACHUSETTS—SOME IN PLYMOUTH IN 1620 AND OTHERS IN SALEM IN 1629. THEY EVENTUALLY BECAME KNOWN AS CONGREGATIONALISTS BECAUSE THEY BELIEVED INDIVIDUAL CHURCHES, NOT A LARGER CHURCH COUNCIL, SHOULD MAKE CHURCH DECISIONS. UNTIL THE EARLY 1800S,

CONGREGATIONALISM WAS ONE OF THE MOST COMMON FORMS OF CHRISTIANITY IN NEW ENGLAND.

IN THE LATE 1700S AND EARLY 1800S, RELIGIOUS REVIVALS BECAME POPULAR IN THE UNITED STATES. THESE LARGE OUTDOOR MEETINGS ATTRACTED LARGE CROWDS TO HEAR PASSIONATE MEN PREACH ABOUT THE IMPORTANCE OF ACCEPTING GOD AS THE WAY INTO HEAVEN. REVIVALS WERE ALSO A GOOD WAY TO SPREAD RELIGION AS SETTLERS EXPANDED INTO THE NEW WESTERN TERRITORIES.

Harriet did so well in her studies that Catharine asked her to teach a class. In addition to her role as student *and* teacher, Harriet spent her time writing poetry and plays, drawing, and painting. She shared her religious ideas and tried to convert the other girls at school. She was tutored in French and Italian.

The school expanded beyond the one room above the harness shop. By 1827, it had its own building on Pratt Street in the center of the city. Catharine shared many of the school responsibilities with Harriet. By age seventeen, Harriet had become a full member of the faculty. She taught students oration (formal speaking), as well as her favorite subject: writing.

Harriet's father was offered the position of president at the Lane Theological Seminary in Cincinnati, Ohio. Moving west was very appealing to the two sisters. Catharine had plans for Cincinnati, too. She wanted to open a female college, and she wanted Harriet's help to run it.

When the term ended in the spring of 1832, Harriet and Catharine joined the Beecher family in the move to Cincinnati. Harriet was now twenty-one years old, leaving New England for the first time to travel west.

Chapter 3
Becoming a Writer

The Beechers took a long stagecoach trip, from Boston to New York to Philadelphia, over the Appalachian Mountains to the town of Wheeling in western Virginia, until they reached their new home in Ohio. In the 1830s, the city of Cincinnati was a major port on the Ohio River with many cotton and paper mills.

Catharine and Harriet opened the Western Female Institute in May 1833. Harriet spent her days teaching at the school, helping at her church, and finding moments to write. Soon, Harriet became a published author. She and Catharine wrote *Primary Geography for Children*. The book was an instant success. Only three months after its printing, the book was already into its fourth edition.

The Beecher sisters' success led to an important
invitation to join the Semi-Colon Club. Uncle
Samuel Foote hosted this group in the parlor of his
spacious home. The club was made up of intelligent
men and women of the Cincinnati community
who met to discuss their literary projects.

Many of its members would go on to become
famous scientists, lawyers, generals, poets, and
historians. Samuel P. Chase would become
Chief Justice of the US Supreme Court. Sarah
Worthington Peter would go on to found the

Philadelphia School of Design for Women. Ormsby M. Mitchel became a leading astronomer and a major general in the Civil War.

In November 1833, Harriet brought her New England story "Uncle Lot" to a Semi-Colon meeting. Judge James Hall, a member of the club, was the editor of *Western Monthly Magazine*. He urged Harriet to submit it to his magazine's literary contest. Harriet won easily. She was

CALVIN E. STOWE

awarded a fifty-dollar prize, and her piece was published in the April 1834 edition of the magazine.

At the Semi-Colon Club, Harriet met a fellow New Englander, Calvin E. Stowe. He was a professor at the Lane Seminary, where Lyman Beecher was president.

Calvin was an expert in languages and the history of the Bible. After his wife, Eliza, died of cholera, Harriet and Calvin grew closer. Before long, Calvin proposed to Harriet. Calvin was nine years older, and large and round compared to Harriet's tiny less-than-five-foot frame. Family and friends gathered for the ceremony on January 6, 1836. Harriet described life in their new Walnut Hills home as "tranquil, quiet, and happy."

THE STOWE HOUSE IN CINCINNATI

Only a few months after the wedding, the Lane Seminary sent Calvin to Europe to purchase books. Harriet was pregnant, so she moved in with her father and family while her husband was away. Harriet spent her time writing. She wrote stories and articles for the *Cincinnati Journal*, where her brother Henry was an editor. She wrote for journals and magazines, such as *Western Monthly Magazine, Godey's Lady's Book*, and the *New York Evangelist*. But soon, Harriet had more than just her writing to take up her

time. Her daughters arrived in September 1836—twins that she named Eliza (after Calvin's first wife) and Isabella.

Calvin arrived home with eight crates of books that he had purchased in London, Paris, and Germany. He had a different idea for the girls' names. He wanted the twins to be named after *both* of his beloved wives. They called the girls Eliza Tyler and Harriet Beecher.

Chapter 4
Troubled Times

The trading of slaves from Africa to other countries was a worldwide industry. Slavery came to the United States along with the colonists.

After the American colonies rebelled against England to become their own country, opinions about slavery in America started to change. The North moved away from slave labor, and laws gradually ended slavery in these states. The South felt that without slaves, their cotton industry would never be as profitable. Slaves made up about a third of the South's overall population.

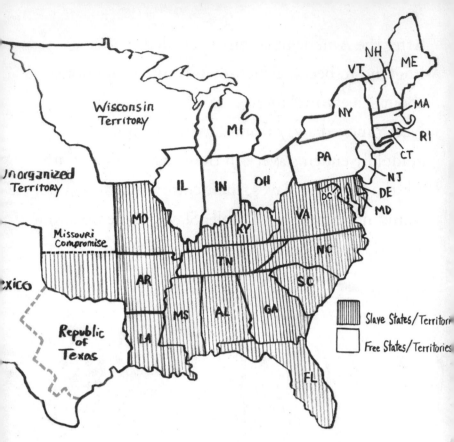

By the late 1830s, a storm was brewing over the issue of slavery in the United States. The country was divided into free states in the North and slave states in the South. Cincinnati was on the border between the free state of Ohio and the slave state Kentucky.

Riots broke out. The city was filled with raging fires and bloody fights.

THE UNDERGROUND RAILROAD

THE UNDERGROUND RAILROAD WAS A SECRET
SYSTEM SET UP TO HELP SLAVES ESCAPE
FROM THE SOUTH TO FREEDOM IN THE NORTH.

IT WAS NOT AN ACTUAL RAILROAD. PEOPLE JUST USED RAILROAD TERMS TO DESCRIBE IT. FUGITIVE SLAVES WOULD TRAVEL FROM "STATION" TO "STATION" ON A ROUTE NORTH WITH THE HELP OF "CONDUCTORS."

STATIONS WERE THE SAFE HOMES OF FREE BLACKS, CHURCH LEADERS, OR NORTHERN ABOLITIONISTS. *CONDUCTORS* WERE THE PEOPLE WHO HELPED LEAD THE SLAVES TO SAFETY. THE JOURNEY WAS DANGEROUS AND DIFFICULT. AFTER SLAVES ESCAPED THEIR PLANTATIONS, THEY TRAVELED BY FOOT, TRAIN, BOAT, AND CART NORTHWARD INTO FREE STATES. SOME EVEN TRAVELED AS FAR AS CANADA.

HARRIET TUBMAN IS ONE OF THE MOST FAMOUS UNDERGROUND RAILROAD CONDUCTORS. SHE WAS RESPONSIBLE FOR LEADING HUNDREDS OF SLAVES TO FREEDOM.

HARRIET TUBMAN

Free blacks in the North were not, however, treated as equals. And even though most Northerners wanted slavery to end, there were disagreements about how that should happen. On one side were abolitionists. They believed that slavery should end immediately. Others supported colonization. They didn't think free blacks would be able to blend with white Americans. They felt slavery should end gradually and that freed blacks should be sent to Africa.

While the topic of slavery gripped the nation, Harriet worked hard to find time to write. She hired servants to help with the children and housekeeping. In the South, slaves were owned by their masters. But servants (or "help") were paid workers. In the North, white help were often immigrants from other countries, such as Germany or Ireland. Black servants were sometimes former slaves.

Harriet couldn't shut herself off from the horror and unfairness of slavery. She expressed a common feeling when she wrote: "No one can have the system of slavery brought before him without an irrepressible desire to *do* something, and what is there to be done?" Many people felt slavery was wrong, but there didn't seem to be a solution. Slavery was so important to the economy of the South that it seemed impossible to get rid of it.

Meanwhile, the Stowe family grew. Harriet gave birth to her son, Henry Ellis Stowe, in 1838. Now with three little children, her life was busy with babies and homemaking. But Harriet wasn't very healthy. She was often in bed feeling ill. When she had another baby boy, Frederick, in 1840, it was a difficult birth.

Harriet had little time for her writing, but she held on to her hopes of becoming an author. In 1842, editors at Harper Brothers publishers in Boston expressed an interest in

publishing a collection of her short stories about New England. So she went east to meet with them. Her short story collection, called *The Mayflower*, was released the following year.

But when Harriet returned to Cincinnati, she was ill, weak, and weary. Her fifth child, Georgiana, was born in August 1843. Harriet had given birth to so many babies in such a short time, Calvin was worried. Her body and spirit seemed to be failing.

Harriet left Cincinnati in March 1846 for the
Brattleboro Water Cure at a medical facility in
Vermont. She didn't return until May of the next
year. She spent her time relaxing and getting well.
Harriet came home refreshed and happy again.
About nine months after she returned, she had a
healthy son, Samuel Charles, in January 1848.
The family called him Charley.

This happiness didn't last long. A cholera epidemic hit Cincinnati during the hot summer of 1849.

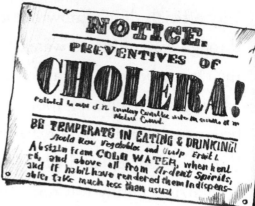

There were so many funerals that the city ran out of hearses to carry the coffins to burial sites. Coffins were transported in uncovered carts designed to carry furniture and other heavy loads.

City officials didn't know that cholera spread through contaminated water. If residents had boiled their water before using it for drinking, cleaning, bathing, and preparing food, many lives might have been saved. By the end of the summer, over eight thousand people had died of cholera in Cincinnati.

Harriet's family was not spared by the cholera epidemic. In early July, baby Charley became ill. In a little more than two weeks, he was dead. Harriet was devastated. Calvin was away in Vermont. She wrote to him: "My Charley—my beautiful, loving, gladsome baby, so loving, so sweet, so full of life and hope and strength—now lies shrouded, pale and cold, in the room below."

When Calvin was offered a job as a professor at Bowdoin College in Brunswick, Maine, Harriet was ready to move. She was eager to return to New England and leave the sadness of Cincinnati behind. Calvin had to finish out his term at Lane Seminary, but Harriet couldn't wait. She was expecting another baby in July 1850, and she didn't want to spend another summer in the city. Brunswick would give her a fresh start.

Chapter 5
Uncle Tom's Cabin

Harriet brought along young Hattie (fourteen), Freddie (ten), and Georgie (seven) to Brunswick. "My head was dizzy with the whirl of railroads and steamboats," she wrote. Fellow travelers mistook them for poor immigrants because of their worn and tattered clothing.

After cleaning, painting, and unpacking, they finally settled into their house on Federal Street.

Calvin and the other two children, Eliza (fourteen) and Henry (thirteen), arrived just in time to greet Charles Edward, another "Charley," who had been born on July 8.

Harriet tackled her life in Maine with a new energy. She started a school in her home for the neighborhood children as well as her own. To save money, she did the housework and cooking herself. She also made time for her writing. She wrote articles regularly for the *National Era*, a weekly newspaper in Washington, DC.

After the Fugitive Slave Law passed in 1850, Harriet was shocked by the stories she heard about black families torn apart as Southerners came north to reclaim their escaped

slaves. She wanted to make a difference.

On a Sunday in February 1851, while she was attending services at the First Parish Church, Harriet had an idea. That same day, Harriet rushed to her bedroom and started writing a scene about a suffering slave. When she read it to her family, they cried.

This scene was just a small part of a larger story she wanted to tell through a series of episodes. Harriet wrote to Mr. Bailey, the editor of the *National Era*, about her idea. She thought the story might be long enough to run each week in three or four issues of the newspaper.

The first episode appeared in the June 5, 1851, issue with the title "Uncle Tom's Cabin, or Life Among the Lowly" by Mrs. H. B. Stowe. Parts of the story appeared every week until April 1, 1852. What started as an idea for only three chapters ended up being forty!

Harriet worked hard to write *Uncle Tom's Cabin*. She collected slave stories. She even wrote to Frederick Douglass (a former slave himself and an important abolitionist leader) to find out what life was like on a cotton plantation.

Harriet faced a new deadline every week. But she never ran out of ideas. She said the story seemed to pour out of her; she felt that God was leading her hand. Over the winter she spent writing *Uncle Tom's Cabin*, she said her heart burst with sadness over the cruelty of slavery. She prayed to God that others would hear her cry to help the slaves.

Uncle Tom's Cabin tells two stories. Both start at the Kentucky plantation of the Shelby family. The Shelbys, who treat their slaves kindly, need to raise money. Mr. Shelby decides to sell his young slave boy Harry. When Harry's mother, Eliza, overhears the plan, she decides they must escape. She does not want to be separated from her son.

The first story follows the slave family northward. Abolitionists help Eliza along the way as she is reunited with her husband and her mother, who have also fled from their masters. Their story has a happy ending.

The second story in *Uncle Tom's Cabin* follows Uncle Tom, the other slave Mr. Shelby decides to sell. Tom is separated from his family and ends up as a slave in New Orleans. His new master is also considerate to Tom, and Tom grows especially close to his owner's daughter, Little Eva St. Clare.

Tom and Eva become good friends. When she becomes ill and dies, her father vows to set Tom free. Sadly, Eva's mother sells Tom to Simon Legree, a cruel master, instead. Legree tortures and beats Tom to death. When George Shelby, the son of Tom's original master, comes to New Orleans to buy Tom back, he is too late.

Thousands of people across the nation in both the North and South read *Uncle Tom's Cabin* in the *National Era*. Many felt moved by the story and shocked by the treatment of slaves.

They couldn't wait for each new installment. Mrs. Jewett, the wife of publisher John P. Jewett of Boston, brought the story to her husband's attention. Jewett offered Harriet a contract to make *Uncle Tom's Cabin* into a book.

FREDERICK DOUGLASS (1818?-1895)

FREDERICK DOUGLASS WAS BORN INTO SLAVERY
IN MARYLAND. AT FIRST, HE WORKED ON A
PLANTATION, BUT THEN WAS SENT TO THE CITY
OF BALTIMORE TO WORK FOR HIS OWNER'S
RELATIVES. IN MARYLAND, FREDERICK LEARNED
HOW TO READ AND WRITE, SOMETHING THAT MOST
MASTERS DID NOT ALLOW THEIR SLAVES TO DO.

FREDERICK RAN AWAY IN 1838 AND MOVED TO MASSACHUSETTS. THERE, LIVING AS A FUGITIVE, HE WENT TO ABOLITIONIST MEETINGS. HE STARTED TO GIVE LECTURES ABOUT HIS LIFE. IN 1845, HE WROTE HIS AUTOBIOGRAPHY, *NARRATIVE OF THE LIFE OF FREDERICK DOUGLASS.* FRIENDS HELPED RAISE MONEY TO BUY HIS FREEDOM SO HE COULD NOT BE BROUGHT BACK TO THE SOUTH AS A SLAVE. HE STARTED AN ABOLITIONIST NEWSPAPER CALLED *THE NORTH STAR.* HE ENCOURAGED BLACK MEN TO SIGN UP AS SOLDIERS TO FIGHT AGAINST THE SOUTH IN THE CIVIL WAR. HE WORKED TIRELESSLY TO HELP BUILD A BRIGHTER FUTURE FOR BLACKS IN AMERICA.

The book was released on March 20, 1852, in two volumes at around the same time the articles ended in the *National Era*. It sold ten thousand copies in its first week and three hundred thousand copies in its first year. In only the first three months, Harriet had earned $10,000.

The *New York Daily Times* of September 18, 1852, reported on Harriet's success. Her income was "the largest sum of money ever received by any author, either American or European, from the sale of a single work in so short a period of time."

Chapter 6
"Tom-mania!"

After *Uncle Tom's Cabin*'s release, Harriet was instantly famous. She was the center of attention at every gathering.

Piles of fan letters awaited her reply. Now that the Stowes had money, they could afford to pay servants, including a housekeeper, a cook, and a governess to help care for her children. The Stowes didn't stay in Brunswick for long. Calvin was offered a job at the Andover Theological Seminary in Andover, Massachusetts. Harriet used some of her earnings to build a new home.

The Stowes bought an old stone structure that had once housed a carpentry shop that made coffins. After it was transformed into the Stowes' new residence, the family called it the Stone Cabin.

Harriet was happy about the move. In a letter to Calvin she wrote, "It seems almost too good to be true that we are going to have such a house in such a beautiful place."

By September, people had written songs and poems based on *Uncle Tom's Cabin*. There were puzzles, toys, and a card game called "Uncle Tom and Little Eva." Fans could buy Tom-themed lamps, dishes, wallpaper, and candlesticks. New York and Boston theater companies performed

plays based on the book. *Uncle Tom's Cabin* was selling well outside the United States, too. It was printed in London. Then editions were released in many other languages, including French, Russian, Italian, Swedish, Portuguese, and German. A newspaper called the popularity of the book "Tom-mania."

Not everyone loved *Uncle Tom's Cabin*. People in the southern United States were outraged. Harriet had thought of the book as a peace

"SIMON LEGREE"

offering to the South. After all, Tom's kind masters were Southerners. Simon Legree, the harshest and most evil slave owner, was originally a Northerner. Little Eva, a Southerner, embraced Tom as an equal.

Harriet had wished to show that not only Southerners and slave owners but also Northerners, cotton investors, and even clergymen were part of the problem. She felt that her book revealed that *everyone* was to blame for the institution of slavery.

Still, Harriet was treated like an enemy. She received letters that called her wicked and threatened to hurt her. It was dangerous to own the book or even display it in bookstores in the South. Children in Richmond, Virginia, chanted a rhyme:

"Go, go, go,
Ol' Harriet Beecher Stowe!
We don't want you here in Virginny—
Go, go, go!"

Harriet wanted to prove to the South that what she wrote was true. She pulled together all the research materials that she had used to write *Uncle Tom's Cabin*, including court cases, slave stories, and her personal experiences. Her new book,

A Key to Uncle Tom's Cabin, came out in 1853. "It is made up of the facts, the documents, the things which my own eyes have looked upon and my hands have handled, that attest this awful indictment upon my country," she wrote.

Harriet then turned her attention to her fans overseas. Slavery had been outlawed in Great Britain and its territories in the 1830s.

Many antislavery groups there continued to spread their message. Groups in Glasgow, Scotland, invited the Stowes to visit England, Ireland, and Scotland. They saw her as a spokeswoman for the antislavery movement in America. Harriet had never traveled so far in her life. Accompanied by Calvin and other family members, she set sail from Boston in April 1853. It was a rough ten-day journey to the port in Liverpool, England.

"Much to my astonishment," she wrote, "I found quite a crowd on the wharf." At first, Harriet wasn't sure why. As her hosts led her to a waiting carriage, the crowd parted. The men took off their hats. The women bowed, smiled, and waved.

They were there to see the tiny woman who
had written such a powerful book. Even as the
carriage drove through the streets of Liverpool,
people came out to catch a glimpse of her
riding by.

Sales of the book in England were more than triple those in the United States. The British applauded Harriet for her attempt to end slavery in America. Harriet toured Britain, stopping to sightsee and appear before antislavery groups.

Tea parties, dinners, and other gatherings were held in her honor. Almost everywhere she went, people cheered for her, stopping to shake her hand or give her flowers. Harriet was treated like a celebrity. Her voice for freedom had reached across the Atlantic and spread through Europe.

Chapter 7
War!

When Harriet returned to the United States in September 1853, her hopes for the country were great. Because of *Uncle Tom's Cabin*, many Americans began to question slavery's place in America. "With regard to the present state of the anti-slavery cause in America," she wrote, "I think, for many reasons, that it has never been more encouraging."

But tensions between the North and South continued to grow. As new territories such as Kansas and Nebraska became states, Congress debated if they should be slaveholding or free. They decided that the new states should decide on their own. So both antislavery and pro-slavery Americans moved into the new states,

hoping to sway the votes. Disagreements between
the two groups became violent.

Harriet's publisher wanted her to write another antislavery book. She agreed. Harriet left on a second voyage to England while her book was still in progress. When the ship arrived in August 1856, she mailed the final manuscript back to Boston with a note to her publisher: "It's done!—and I send it. You may have it published as soon as you please."

Harriet was still in London when *Dred: A Tale of the Great Dismal Swamp* was released. It did not get the same wonderful reviews that *Uncle Tom's Cabin* had. But Harriet was pleased when she heard the news that Queen Victoria had read *Dred* and liked it even more.

Harriet traveled throughout Europe for almost a year, returning home in June 1857. Soon after,

Harriet received a telegram with horrifying news. Her son Henry, a student at Dartmouth College in New Hampshire, had drowned while swimming. Harriet's grief was great, but not even this tragedy could weaken her desire to end slavery. She realized her loss must be similar to what slave mothers felt when their families were torn apart, sold, and separated from one another.

Harriet spent her time writing, using the joys and sadness in her life as inspiration for her work. While Harriet wrote, tensions in the country exploded into war. Abraham Lincoln had been elected president in 1860. By this time, there were about four million slaves in the South. The Southern slave states decided to separate from the rest of the country.

ABRAHAM LINCOLN

They wanted to continue to buy and own slaves. They called themselves the Confederate States of America. President Lincoln wanted to keep the country unified. He also wanted to end slavery.

The war between the Union (North) and the Confederacy (South) officially began on April 12, 1861, when Confederates fired on Union soldiers at Fort Sumter in Charleston, South Carolina.

In Andover, Massachusetts, young men on the seminary campus marched and trained as soldiers. Women sewed red braids onto blue flannel shirts for use as uniforms. Harriet's own son Fred enlisted for the Union Army. When he headed for the front lines, Harriet saw him off at the Jersey City train depot.

In 1862, President Abraham Lincoln drafted the Emancipation Proclamation. This official

document would grant freedom to the slaves living in the Southern states at war. The law would not go into effect until January 1, 1863. Harriet wanted to make sure that this news wasn't too good to be true. She wanted to meet the president herself. Harriet headed to the capital. "I am going to Washington," she wrote, "to see the heads of departments myself."

On December 2, 1862, Harriet met President Lincoln in a cozy room before a fire in the White House. She said that he greeted her with a twinkle in his eye, saying, "So you're the little woman who wrote the book that made this great war!" Then they sat and chatted. Harriet decided that her hopes might come true. She could trust Lincoln to end slavery.

On New Year's Day 1863, Harriet was attending a concert at the Boston Music Hall when a man walked on stage. He announced that President Lincoln had signed the Emancipation Proclamation. The audience cheered. Harriet heard people chanting, "Mrs. Stowe! Mrs. Stowe!" She stood, tears in her eyes, to accept their thanks.

Chapter 8
Home in Hartford

The American Civil War finally ended when the Confederates surrendered to the Union in April 1865.

The southern states that had broken away were part of the United States once again. The war had raged on for four years in clashes both on land and at sea. Almost three quarters of a million people died in the Civil War—more Americans than in any other war in history. Slavery, however, was over, once and for all.

Southerners, both
former slave owners and former slaves,
had to start building a new way of life.

As the war was drawing to an end, Calvin retired from the Andover Theological Seminary. The family built a new home in Hartford, where Harriet had spent her teenage years. Harriet started writing about household subjects. Her column "House and Home Papers" in the *Atlantic Monthly* discussed topics such as cooking, cleaning, decorating, and how to make a welcoming home. Harriet also wrote stories for the children's magazine *Our Young Folks*.

For so many years, Harriet had not been welcome in the South. But in 1868, the Stowes purchased a second home in Florida to get away from the cold winters of New England. They were building a new life, too. The healthy air of Mandarin, Florida, smelled like oranges from the nearby grove. Harriet worked to raise money to establish churches and schools for black families in the community.

Harriet was almost sixty and still a famous

and successful writer. She split her time between
Hartford and Mandarin. Her book of New
England stories based on Calvin's childhood in
Massachusetts, *Oldtown Folks*, came out in 1869.
She continued to write articles and novels. Soon,
Harriet wanted to settle back in Hartford full
time. The Stowes decided to buy a smaller house
on Forest Street.

Harriet visited with friends, admirers, and reporters in the parlor; wrote letters; and enjoyed the company of her eldest daughters, who lived at home and had never married. Harriet tended to her garden and found time to paint, both hobbies she took pleasure in her entire life.

The editors of the *Atlantic Monthly* had a tradition of celebrating the seventieth birthdays of their famous authors. They planned a big party for Harriet. But they missed her actual birthday by a year. The celebration was held in 1882—the summer she turned seventy-one!

About two hundred guests came to the garden party held on a country estate outside Boston. They gave speeches and read poems in Harriet's honor. Harriet also gave a speech. She wanted the guests to remember what was most important to her: "If any one of you have doubt, or sorrow, or pain—if you doubt about this world, just remember what God has done.

Just remember that this great sorrow of slavery has gone, has gone forever."

In 1886, Harriet's dear husband, Calvin, passed away. Harriet spent her days taking walks and enjoying her home. She didn't write much anymore. Her mind wasn't as sharp. "My mind wanders like a running brook," she explained to a friend. "My sun has set. The time of work for *me* is over. I have written all my words and thought all my thoughts."

As Harriet approached the last chapter of her own life, she began to think about how she would be remembered. So she started sifting through all of her papers and letters. She asked her son Charles to write a biography of her, and they worked on it together until it was completed in 1889.

When Harriet was eight-five years old, on July 1, 1896, she quietly passed away in her bed. A few days later, she was buried in Andover, Massachusetts, in a plot between Calvin and her son Henry. The *New York Times* reported on the death of a woman they called a "genius."

In her lifetime, Harriet had not only written words in newspapers, magazines, and books. She had also written about her hopes to end slavery in her nation and the world. She was grateful for her successes in life. In one of her last letters to a friend, she wrote, "Blessed I have been in many ways, in seeing many of the desires of my heart fulfilled."

Harriet's final home in Hartford, Connecticut, now houses the Harriet Beecher Stowe Center. Visitors can take tours of the parlors, workspaces, and bedrooms, filled with Harriet's treasures, paintings, and Uncle Tom memorabilia. The center hopes to inspire visitors toward action for equality and social justice in their own communities.

TIMELINE OF
HARRIET BEECHER STOWE'S LIFE

1811	Harriet Beecher is born in Litchfield, Connecticut, on June 14
1832	Moves with the Beecher family to Cincinnati, Ohio, where she teaches at the Western Female Institute
1833	*Primary Geography for Children,* by coauthors Harriet and Catharine Beecher, is published Both sisters join the Semi-Colon Club
1836	Marries Calvin Stowe on January 6 They are joined by twin daughters Eliza and Harriet in September
1838	Son Henry is born
1840	Son Frederick is born
1843	*The Mayflower,* a collection of Harriet's stories, is published Daughter Georgiana is born
1848	Son Samuel Charles (Charley) is born
1849	Charley dies of cholera
1850	The family moves to Brunswick, Maine Son Charles is born
1851-1852	*Uncle Tom's Cabin* appears in the *National Era*; it is later published as a book in March 1852
1852	The Stowes move to Andover, Massachusetts
1853	*The Key to Uncle Tom's Cabin* is published Harriet goes on her first trip to Europe
1856	*Dred: A Tale of the Great Dismal Swamp* is published
1857	Son Henry drowns
1864	Moves to Hartford, Connecticut
1896	Dies in Hartford and is buried in Andover, Massachusetts

TIMELINE OF THE WORLD

Eli Whitney invents the cotton gin, which leads to a booming economy in the South — **1793**

The War of 1812 is fought between the British and the United States over trade issues — **1812**

The Savannah is the first steam-powered ship to cross the Atlantic Ocean — **1819**

The Erie Canal is completed, connecting the Great Lakes to the Atlantic Ocean — **1825**

French artist Louis Daguerre creates the daguerreotype, the first form of photography — **1839**

Frederick Douglass, famous abolitionist and escaped slave, publishes his autobiography *Narrative of the Life of Frederick Douglass* — **1845**

The first postage stamps are used to send letters in the United States — **1847**

The First Women's Rights Convention is held in Seneca Falls, New York — **1848**

British naturalist Charles Darwin publishes his ideas of evolution in his book *On the Origin of Species* — **1859**

North and South fight in the American Civil War — **1861-1865**

The first transcontinental railroad is completed in America, connecting the nation from east to west — **1869**

Alexander Graham Bell invents the telephone — **1876**

Thomas Edison invents the electric lightbulb — **1879**

The Eiffel Tower is built as the entrance for the World's Fair in Paris — **1889**

The United States passes the Nineteenth Amendment, giving women the right to vote — **1920**

BIBLIOGRAPHY

Fields, Annie (ed.). **Life and Letters of Harriet Beecher Stowe**. Boston: Houghton, Mifflin and Company, 1897.

Hedrick, Joan D. **Harriet Beecher Stowe: A Life**. New York: Oxford University Press, 1994.

Johnston, Johanna. **Runaway to Heaven: The Story of Harriet Beecher Stowe**. Garden City, New York: Doubleday, 1963.

Stowe, Charles Edward. **Harriet Beecher Stowe: The Story of Her Life**. Boston and New York: Houghton Mifflin Company, 1911.

Stowe, Harriet Beecher. **Uncle Tom's Cabin**. Oxford: Oxford University Press, 2011.

Wilson, Forrest. **Crusader in Crinoline: The Life of Harriet Beecher Stowe**. Philadelphia: J.B. Lippincott and Company, 1941.